THE PURPLE PIG

JENNIFER HENGY
ILLUSTRATED BY JENNIFER HENGY

xulon PRESS

Once upon a time, on a faraway hill, there lived a herd of pigs.
There were pink pigs, black and white pigs and orange pigs.
The pink pigs loved to gaze all day into the pond on top of the hill and look at
how beautiful they were.
The black and white pigs loved to gaze at the stars in the night sky and
talk about really smart things.
The orange pigs loved to roll down the hill and see who could make it back
to the top the fastest.
Every day was perfect for each type of piggy,
except for one lonely little pig,
the purple pig.

He would try to look at himself in the pond with the pink pigs but they crowded the pond so he could not look in.

The purple pig tried to lay on his back at night and gaze at the stars in the sky with the black and white pigs. But they talked about such smart things, the purple pig didn't understand what they were talking about.

He would even roll down the hill with the orange pigs but they were so fast when they ran back up the hill the dust that they kicked up blinded him. He was always left at the bottom of the hill with tears in his eyes.

So every day, the purple pig would lay at the very edge of the forest that surrounded the hill and watch the other piggy's play.

One night, the purple pig decided to leave. He felt so alone and only wanted to have a friend.

He wandered through the forest, over the next hill and down into a valley.

He wandered all through the night.

The little piggy was sad and tired and tired of being sad.

The purple pig laid down by a lily pond.

He started to cry and couldn't stop. The tears just kept coming and rolled down his snout and hit the edge of the pond sending ripples through the water.

In the lily pond on top of one of the lilies, there lived a fairy.

The fairy heard the purple pig crying and flew over to him.

"Why are you crying little pig?" asked the fairy.

"I am so sad" said the purple pig. "No one wants to be my friend. The pink pigs are too beautiful to be my friend. I don't understand what the black and white pigs are talking about and the orange pigs don't want me to run and play with them. I only want to have a friend."

He laid his head back down on the cool grass and started to cry all over again.

"Stop crying little pig. I am a fairy and I am going to grant you three wishes."

The purple pig lifted his head in surprise, "Really?" The little pig jumped for joy.

"Oh I know exactly what I am going to wish for! For my first wish, I wish I were a pink pig. Just as beautiful as all the other pink pigs in the herd."

"Ok" said the fairy and with that, she waved her wand and instantly the purple pig was no longer purple, but PINK!

The little pig jumped in the air and spun around. He was so excited and happy that he squealed with delight.

"Oh thank you! Thank you!" he told the fairy. The fairy smiled and flew back to her lily pad. The little pig ran all the way back to the herd he had left.

In the morning when the other pink pigs were waking up to go to the pond, the purple pig, who was no longer purple, joined them.

"Oh you are so beautiful" said one of the pink pigs to him. "Here, look into the pond with us and see for yourself."

The little pig squeezed himself next to the other pink pigs and looked into the pond.

He was beautiful! He looked and looked into the pond and smiled at what he saw. The purple pig who was no longer purple was the happiest he had been in his whole piggy life!

But as the day went on, the little pig began to feel sad again.

The pink pigs didn't talk to each other. They looked into the pond all day and when one pig turned his head away the others would laugh and make fun of that pig.

Did the purple pig really want friends like this? "I don't want to be a pink pig if they only make fun of each other! That's not what a friend does."

So he made up his mind that he would leave that night while the other pigs were sleeping. He would go back to the fairy and ask for his second wish.

The purple pig wandered through the forest, over the next hill and down into a valley.

He wandered all through the night until he found the lily pond where the fairy lived.

"Fairy? Are you there?" asked the purple pig who was no longer purple.

"Of course I am!" said the fairy as she stood up on her lily pad and flew towards him.

"Tell me what is wrong?"

"I am so sad" said the purple pig as a tear rolled down his snout.
"The pink pigs are very beautiful but they only make fun of each other when their backs are turned. I don't want to make fun of others for things they cannot change!
I want to have a true friend."
He laid his head back down on the cool grass and continued to cry.
"Stop crying little pig. Remember, you still have two wishes left."
The purple pig lifted his head and said "Yes I know." He thought about
what he wanted for his second wish.
"For my second wish I would like to be a black and white pig. I would like to gaze at the stars in the night sky and be just as smart as all the other black and white pigs. I know they will not make fun of each other. They are so smart, they surely know
what it is to be true friends."
The fairy waved her wand and instantly the purple pig was
no longer pink but black and white!
The little pig jumped in the air and spun around. He was so excited
and happy that he squealed with delight.
"Oh thank you! Thank you!" He told the fairy.
The fairy smiled and flew back to her lily pad.
The little pig ran all the way back to the herd he had left.
It was still night when the little pig reached the herd.
The pink and orange pigs were fast asleep but the black and white pigs were
staring at the stars and deep in talk.
The little pig sat down next to them.
He knew exactly what they were talking about!

He joined them in conversation and soon all the black and
white pigs knew who this pig was.
The little pig had never been prouder of himself!
But as the sun came up, he became sad again.
The little pig wandered down the hill and laid down at the edge of the forest all by himself.
"Those black and white pigs are very smart indeed. They really do know everything about
everything... except for one thing. I thought because they talked to each other all of the
time they would be best friends! But they are so focused on knowing more than the pig
next to them, they never learn about the pig next to them. They are not friends at all!"
He decided that he would leave the herd for the second night in a row.
The little pig would return to the fairy for his third and final wish.
The purple pig who was no longer purple, wandered through the forest,
over the next hill and down into a valley.
He wandered all through the night until he found the lily pond where the fairy lived.
"Fairy? Are you there?" asked the purple pig who was no longer purple.
"Of course I am! Tell me what is wrong?" said the fairy as she flew towards him.
"I am so sad" said the purple pig as a tear rolled down his snout.
"The black and white pigs are truly very smart but they don't care how each other feels.
They know everything about everything but know nothing about each other! I want a real
friend - a friend who knows everything about me. One that I can laugh and play with."
He laid his head back down on the cool grass and continued to cry.

"Stop crying little pig. Remember you still have one wish left" said the fairy.
The little pig thought for a long time.
So long in fact, that the fairy had to rest her wings and sit on the little pig's snout.
She was worried about the little pig's heart and how broken it was.
The kind fairy hoped he made the right wish on his last try.
He stopped crying and smiled at the fairy.
"OK I know what my last wish will be" said the purple pig who was no longer purple
as the fairy started to fly again.
"For my third and final wish, I wish to be an orange pig. I want to be as fast as all the other
orange pigs. I know they must be true friends as they play and laugh together all day."
The fairy smiled down at the little pig. She shrugged her shoulders and hoped he would find
what he was looking for as she waved her wand.
Instantly the purple pig was no longer black and white but orange!
The little pig jumped in the air and spun around. He was so excited and
happy that he squealed with delight.
"Oh thank you! Thank you!" he told the fairy. The fairy smiled and flew back to her lily pad.
The little pig ran all the way back to the herd that he had left.
When he reached the hill, the orange pigs were just about to roll down it.
They saw him and called for the little piggy to join them.
The herd of orange pigs all rolled down the hill together.

The purple pig who was no longer purple, laughed so hard as the grass tickled his belly.
He never knew rolling down the hill could be so much fun!
When they reached the bottom, all the other orange pigs began
to get ready to race to the top.
The purple pig joined the other orange pigs as they began to paw at the dirt.
And just as the little pig blinked his eyes, the orange piggy's were off!
They are so fast thought the little pig! He chased after them and was able to reach the
herd just as they started to climb the hill!
He was grinning from ear to ear!
But this did not last long!
Instead of running up the hill and seeing who was the fastest,
the orange pigs shoved and pushed each other on the way to the top.
These pigs were not friends!
Friends would not hurt each other and fight like these pigs were doing!
The little pig stopped dead in his tracks. He never knew that this is what happened
with the orange pigs. When he was purple he never made it this far because the dust
from all the pig's running always got in his eyes and he couldn't see.
The purple pig turned away from the other orange pigs and with a very heavy heart,
returned to his spot on the edge of the forest.
He had never been so sad in all of his life.
The little pig didn't know what to do!

He had used his last wish with the fairy at the pond and knew he would remain a mean orange pig for the rest of his life.
The purple pig who was purple no more was lonelier now than when he was purple!
How could this be? he thought to himself.
He thought for sure if he was any color other than purple he would have all the piggy friends he wanted.
The little pig made up his mind right then that he would leave for good. He would go live on his own, alone and friendless forever.
The little pig wandered through the forest, over the next hill and down into a valley.

He wandered and wandered – he wandered all day until he realized he was lost.
He had no idea where he was and knew that night was fast approaching.
The little pig turned around and went back the way he came.
He wandered up one hill and down another.
It was very dark. He found himself back in a forest but the sounds of a forest at night are very scary. The little pig needed to get out of this forest and fast!
He could only think of one thing to do - he closed his eyes and ran.
He ran and ran as fast as he could!

But you and I both know that you don't get very far running with your eyes closed!
The purple pig found himself falling and rolling fast down a hill!
He rolled faster and faster when all of a sudden…SPLASH!!!!!
The little pig found himself lying face first in a pond with a lily pad on his head.
The purple pig, who was no longer purple, picked himself up
and began to shake the water off.
He was so cold, so wet and so lonely. He didn't just start to cry, he started to BAWL!!!
The little pig bawled and bawled and bawled.
He bawled so loud that everything in the forest became quiet —
he even woke the fairy who lived in the lily pond.
The fairy rubbed her tired eyes and yawned.
She had an idea who was making all of the raucous.
She stood up on her lily pad and flew over to the purple pig, who was no longer purple.
She landed on his snout.
The little pig opened his eyes with a start and immediately stopped bawling.
The fairy looked deep into the little pigs eyes. She wiped a tear away
from his cheek and smiled.
"Why are you crying little pig" asked the fairy.

The little pig sighed and sat up with the fairy still perched on his nose.
"I am going to be a mean orange pig forever. I have used up all of my wishes and I never made any friends with the other pigs. I thought being beautiful like the pink pigs would make me happy but it didn't. I thought being super smart and having lots of smart friends would make me happy but none of the black and white pigs are friends. I thought rolling down the hill with the orange pigs would be so much fun. I realize now, that all they want to do is win no matter who they hurt on their way to the top."
The fairy sat on the little pig's snout for a long time.
She knew that the purple pig, who was no longer purple had learned a valuable lesson.
"Ok my little friend. I will give you one last wish. Choose very wisely as this truly is your last wish."

The little pig looked up at the fairy, eyes full of joy. He knew exactly what he was going to wish for.
"Please fairy, make me purple again."
The fairy smiled.
She waved her wand and the little orange pig was now the purple pig again!

The little pig jumped in the air and spun around. He was so excited and happy and squealed with delight.
"Oh thank you! Thank you!" He told the fairy.
"I know that it is not what you look like on the outside but who you are on the inside that counts. Treating others as you want to be treated is the only way to be. If I am happy with myself, then it doesn't matter what the other pigs think of me - I will be happy no matter what!
You have given me the greatest gift - to be myself again!"

And with that, the purple pig ran through the forest and back to the herd of pink, black and white and orange pigs.
The herd was just beginning to stir when the little pig arrived at the top of the hill.

He reached the pink pigs first and smiled at them.
"Good morning pink pigs" said the purple pig.

The pink pigs all turned to him and said "Where have you been purple pig?"
"I ran away to see if I could find a different herd to live with.
I was so lonely and no one would be my friend."
The pink pigs stared at the purple pig with their mouths wide open.
"We thought you were the most beautiful pig of all" said one of the pink pigs.
"No other pig in the whole herd is purple. All pigs know that purple is the color of kings. You never spoke to us and we thought you were too beautiful to talk to.
Every day when we look into the pond, we hold our breath and try to turn purple. We couldn't speak to each other and would let out a gasp when we needed to breathe. We wanted so much to be as beautiful as you, we would laugh at one another's attempts."
The purple pig was shocked!
They thought he was beautiful? They wanted to be like him? He never knew!

He smiled at the pink pigs and said to them "You are beautiful. You should never want to change the color of your skin. You are perfect just the way you are. Thank you for letting me know. We will be friends from now on."

The pink pigs were so delighted by this that they jumped and squealed in delight.

The purple pig jumped with them and laughed.

If the pink piggy's thought this of him, what did the other pigs think?

He had to find out.

So the purple pig left the pink pigs to meet the next group.

"Off to bed?" asked the purple pig to the first black and white pig he met.

"Oh yes purple pig. We are tired of looking at the stars and talking all night. We still do not know the answer to our life long question. Oh well, maybe tomorrow"

the pig said as he turned to go.

"May I ask what the question is?" asked the purple pig.

The black and white pig stopped and turned around.

"The question is, what is the true meaning of happiness?" said the black and white pig to the purple pig as all the other black and white pigs joined the conversation.

"I believe the true meaning of happiness is to be happy with one's self. Don't worry about what others say. If you believe in yourself you can do anything. Happiness comes from within. You only need to look into your heart to find it" replied the purple pig.

The black and white pigs all looked at each other in amazement.

They could not believe this purple pig, a pig whom had never shared any super smarts words with them before knew something they had been trying to understand forever.
"Would you come tomorrow night and have more super smart talks with us?"
asked one of the black and white pigs.
"We would love to hear more from you. We have been puzzling over
this question forever and you have answered it in just a minute."
"Of course! I would love to" said the little pig.
"Thank you our friend" said the white and black pigs. "We are so tired now
from our super smart talks and need to go to bed."
"See you tomorrow night" and with that the purple pig wandered off
in search of the orange pigs.
The orange pigs were just about to start rolling down the hill.
"Wait up!" exclaimed the purple pig.
The orange pigs all turned around to see who had spoken.
"Did you want to join us purple pig? We were about to start our game"
said one of the orange piggy's.
"I would really like to play but I don't want to be shoved and pushed
when I run back up the hill" said the purple pig.
"Shoved and pushed?" asked one of the orange pigs. There was a moment of
silence before one of the orange piggy's spoke up again.
"Oh you mean when we push each other so that we don't fall into the holes that
we have created from running super-fast up the hill?
If one of us fell into a hole we would definitely twist a hoof."

The purple pig started to laugh.
"Is that what you were doing? I thought you were shoving and
pushing each other to get to the top first and win."
"No!" said one of the orange pigs.
"We don't care who wins as long as we all have fun along the way and we don't get hurt.
So… do you want to roll down the hill and have the grass tickle your belly?"
"I would love to" said the purple pig with a smile.
He lined up with all the orange pigs and began rolling down the hill.
The little pig loved the way the grass tickled!
He laughed all the way to the bottom of the hill.
Today was the happiest day of his piggy life. The purple pig -
who was so glad he was purple - had found all the friends he could possibly want.
This purple pig would never be lonely again.

CPSIA information can be obtained
at www.ICGtesting.com
Printed in the USA
LVOW02s2039310516
490669LV00002B/2/P